TAX-FREE PHRASES

TAX-FREE PHRASES

Poems

Michael Maiello

Beckham
Publications Group, Inc.
Silver Spring

Published in the United States by
Beckham Publications Group, Inc.
P.O. Box 4066, Silver Spring, MD 20914

ISBN: 978-0-9984870-8-3

Library of Congress Control Number: 2017938917

CONTENTS

PART ONE: JUMP STARTS

PART TWO: MOTION LESS

PART THREE: RITES AND WRONGS

PART ONE

JUMP STARTS

ROCKETEERS

Kennedy, Castro and Khrushchev have gone.
So has my wife and job.
But the bar I'm sitting at
and have sat at remains.
Bartenders change, the price of shots changes
and I have changed as well.
I drink more in less time
and remember less more.
The market for fallout shelters is definitely down.
My broker calls to remind me
we won the space race.

KING

Revolutions are chapters of a book never finished.
French, American, Russian, Cuban,
the rebels convene to draft declarations.
It seems there must always be declarations.
There once were Students For A Democratic Society.
Is there, has there ever been one?
Now that a black man is president of the nation
we might believe there was a dream yesterday.

WAR FARE

My godfather was awarded three Purple Hearts
during World War Two.
He ordered me to throw them away
upon his expiration.
The man had a lot of heart
and a disarming disinterest in decoration.

LIE SENSE

You need a license to marry,
a license to divorce,
a license to hunt, a license to fish,
a license to work, a license to retire,
a license to prove you are disabled.
If hell is a license bureau,
heaven is eternal freedom from it.

PRISON PERSPECTIVE

If you spend time in prison you learn
some gospel truths:
All men are created unequal.
No one is guilty of anything.
Guards guard themselves.
It's good not to be attractive.
Upon release you will also learn
that cell sizes differ, that's all.

PENTECOSTAL PARADES

Leafless trees are prayers to the future.
Autumn is their Pentecost, dead saints their patrons.
The wealthy lead parades to parties
where bishops will baptize their children.
The children are named after saints
who never knew they were saintly.
That would be a sin of pride.
Later the children will learn to be proud.

MANHATTAN MEDITATION

The center of the universe is any point
from which you observe its expansion.
Your center is where you forget you are.
Travel agents guarantee both can be reached
on vacation but landlords insist on receiving rent first.
The chanting of prayers can also help
if pigeons and pedestrians in their ways recite
and elevators give way to elevation.

T B

Fidel has been consumed by age and ideology.
The sixties students were consumed by consumption.
An awkward lion is consumed by his pride.
I am consumed by campaigning for election
to the presidency of Easter Island
(on the Resurrection Party ticket).
Remember, it's your consummate duty to vote.

THE LONG TENT MEETING

After five hundred years of the white man's intrusion
the Iroquois elders met to ponder whether or not
it had to be this way.
They conferred in the long tent, abstaining
from food and drink until emerging
with the enigmatic answer: Yes.
Many were later awarded honorary
doctorates in history.

SOUTH BRONX BLUES

I've spent the day reading the grandeur of graffiti
and realizing life is always in midair.
Civilization means joints and pizza
and looking to the future with some degree
of confidence it will become the past.
So I'm only partly civilized.
The question was raised at a community meeting.

SIGHS ASIDE

The full moon is chanting
a painful psalm
about being stepped on
and forgotten.
When I stop listening,
I hear the melody,
every now and Zen.

HAVANA GRAND SLAMS

The dream of exporting our famous
revolution is over.
Karl who? Fidel who?
We want to be friends with the United States.
That's where the best baseball is played.
That's the best market for cigars.
We want computers and Santana concerts.
We want to vacation in Miami.
Guerillas don't make war.
They make love in zoos.
What were the last words of Che Guevara?
What's the batting average of anyone who cares?

VOCATIONS

Friends are drinking coffee in the back of the garage
making comments on the history of the world.
They consider starting a cult that celebrates
property rites.
It would recognize no sins or require contributions
and would sponsor Holy Land tours
of the World Bank and Wall Street.
Devils would be tax collectors,
angels renegade accountants.
It's been ages since I've been
in some kind of trouble.
Time spent in purgatory.

MA BELL

When you're drunk you forget that music
and memories can't be grasped.
So a drunk down the bar keeps humming
and reaching for his ex.
There's a ringing in my ears that sounds
familiar.
it means world integrity may well require
the mass destruction of telephones.
The bartender's pretending for sake
of friendship
that it's not near closing time.
He knows I want to believe him.

YELLOWSTONED

Everything alive will pass.
It's nature's way of saying it's dependable.
So trees and brooks need not conspire
against cars and tents and campers.
They just grow and flow and wait
while staff attend to parking lots.

GROUND ZERO

I've been offered an appointment to the committee
that names lunar craters.
There are hundreds of unnamed craters
and hundreds of unused names.
Matches will require a grace found in church
and an equal level of solemn inactivity.
I'm considering accepting, noting even coffee
grounds once produced something.
The local paper will cite the honor, to occur
some light weeks away.
History in the making.
Sanity in the baking.

BLACK OUT

Waves massage an invisible beach
while light bulbs grow jealous of candles.
Saints smile at us
from the side
of the moon
no one ever
sees.

THE COLD PEACE

There are people proud to have been part
of the counter counter culture.
They believe they saved the nation
from the spoiled ideas of their spoiled children.
Long hair and peace signs meant subversion
and the crazy music only made everyone crazy.
They are so glad the whole thing is over.
A generation that cannot dream
without the threat of war.
They had cold war. They have cold peace.
The always cold truce between brothers.

PART TWO

MOTION LESS

MEMORIAL DAYS

We're heating the planet,
trashing the oceans
and buying Japanese cars.
Veterans of Okinawa
testified to Congress
that the last is beyond
doubt the worse.

EVENING EVENINGS

Evenings pass like weather and good intentions
as we wait...for messages from the planets of stars
thousands of light beers away.

SIGNS

This morning I gave a peace sign to the sanitation men
who were loading their truck.
They signed me back.
This verifies our mutual understanding of garbage.
It has a beauty all its own
that emanates from being disposed of.
The beauty of no longer being possessed.
Peace.

STORMED

The *Wall Street Journal* advises investing in snow.
After all, you can always anticipate low temperatures
some time during the year.
Temperatures that will engender weather
that will engender snow.
Snow removal creates jobs that bolster the economy.
We might even be able to create the conditions
that create snow.
Should that happen, prepare for soaring stocks
that take the market by storm.

LANDINGS

We spent billions putting men on the moon.
To take great photos?
To bring back rocks and dust?
To be one up on the Russians?
Money that could have fed hungry people.
Built homes and schools where there were none.
Perhaps even cured a disease.
But we needed press and propaganda.
Because those were the times
that tried men's souls
and that's what our souls
chose to try.

ARMISTICE

I spent most of the day in a hunting stand
waiting for a white tail to pass by.
It was almost evening when a buck, barely antlered,
finally did.
He looked at me and saw nothing.
I saw, then sighted him in.
I did nothing more and he walked on.
I understood my killing days were over.
I can buy what meat I need
at Shop Rite and prove my virility
telling lies about the hunt.
With a little luck my buck will prove
his too
and tell lies about it to his fawn.
Long winters made longer.

LONERS

After eons of Divine indifference my lover's
leaving doesn't mean that much.
Where to score marijuana is the issue.
Additional critical concerns:
Who is the Godfather?
Where are Marlon Brando and Al Pacino
when you need them?
When was the last lunar landing
and who was it that landed?
My doctor died from disinterested
interest returns.
A case of declining economic health.
So this year vacation in New York,
the quality Loan Star State.

THE ELECT

The men who left Vietnam say
"Live and let live" is a great idea
for people who are still alive.
They meet yearly because they know
those who have killed know
only other killers really know.
Time passes and they become as rare
as pacifist piranhas.
A species whose members lost the right
to vote.

OUTDOOR EXHIBITIONS

At least twice a year I go back to the Bronx
to ponder the grandeur of graffiti.
An art of anger created on the run.
An art of concrete expression.
It asks who knows the dignity
of those the moneyed say have none?
Perhaps the artists smoking grass
at the Bronx Botanical Gardens
and retired jazz musicians
recalling just the right rifts.

SCOTCH AND WATER

At what point are we disillusioned?
Health found, health lost?
Love found, love lost?
Faith found, faith lost?
When you sweep away tall tales
and vanity, what's left?
Scotch whiskey on the rocks
and a vanishing view of the Hudson.

EQUAL RIGHTS

Eastern Europeans, Africans, Asians, Polynesians,
Eskimos, Indians, American Indians, the poor
and the poor in spirit.
Is there anyone we have failed to dislike
and take advantage of?
Yes, Greenlanders, I believe.
We must reach out to them at once
or put at risk the profit
from the fish they fish.

LEONIDAS AND THE HUNG OVER SPARTANS

It's been a long night in a lot of bars
with a lot of short people I'm sure
not to remember.
A long morning is probably at hand as well.
What do you do when you wake up drunk
with a "for sale" sign on your head?
You howl at the moon.
You howl at the sun.
You howl at your whole family
and dare the Persians
to pass through the pass.

EXPEDITIONS

There's the Appalachian Trail and the
Bronx River Parkway.
Both require valid passports and proof
of good intention.
The natives exchange whiskey and grass
for valid currency and can be violent
if exploited.
They speak languages that are only now
beginning to be fully understood.
Upon return you might write a book
describing the adventure or be featured
in an issue of *National Geographic*.
Where now to go? Confession?

SIGHS ASIDE

The full moon is chanting
a painful psalm
about being stepped on
and forgotten.
When I stop listening,
I hear the melody,
every now and Zen.

ROCKS AND ROLES

The castles in England are cold.
Very cold.
They have survived war bombing,
the erosion of weather and birds.
But now their ghosts have fled
for fear of tourists.
They turn steadfastly towards the future
as have the monarchy and the Rolling Stones.
This is history and must not be forgotten.
This stage for beer and Shakespeare
and actors seeking audience.

NICE

There is really a town in southern
New York named Pleasantville.
If I lived there I'd refuse to pay taxes.
That would be pleasant.
If I lived there I would try to be pleasant.
That would not.
Where do birds retire and deer vacation?
Pleasantville, of course.

A VOID

Democrats, Republicans, Conservatives, Liberals,
Socialists, Feminists, Anarchists.
What's missing is a Party Party
where everyone gets high at the convention.
Employment will cease.
Benefits will begin.
The need for elections will be over.

PROPHECY

The world will end when everyone fasts
until the Second Coming
which for reasons unknown has been
seemingly indefinitely postponed.
So, vacation tours of Patmos
presently appear providential.
They're good for you, good for me,
good for the economy.

DESCENDING

Why do we say "fallen in love"
instead of "risen to love"?
There's something ominous about the former,
is there not?
We fall down, we fall short, we fall over,
we fall for, we falter.
Positive connotations are missing here.
Success is possible. I once achieved it,
but I've been happier since I fell.

PART THREE

RITES AND WRONGS

NO RESERVATIONS

What happens when the only forests are federal and
the only Indians are from Cleveland?
You breathe conditioned air and search for pools to swim in
and organize hunting parties to distant sales events.

THIS HOLY DAY

My four-year-old grandson wants a model jet fighter for Christmas.
His parents will surprise him with this gift.
Peace, good will and combat fantasies to all.
Wise men are journeying to shopping malls in the East.
Prophecies of discounts and bargains abound.

COMMITTED

I'm bored submitting requests for probation.
It's like celebrating posthumous birthdays
and watching Super Bowl reruns.
You know what's going to happen
before the play is run.
It's like playing saxophone in daylight.
The mystery is lost.
Friday night the inmates shooting craps
admitted they miss the Cold War.
Fidel Castro, aged and forgotten,
hits home runs in his dreams
and persecutes Yankee fans.
He misses the Cold War.
I'm reading biographies of Mao Tse-Tung
and Joe Di Maggio.
Trying to miss my cell.

THAT'S OLD, MAN

When the pool you go to is on a table
and the island you sail to is Staten
and the woman you're dining with never heard
of Bob Dylan,
then you possess the priceless sixth sense
that permits you to tactfully make none.

IFOS

Life is a series of verified reports
of identified flying objects,
most of which have permanently landed.

THE DEPTHS OF PROFESSION

One of my sons is an attorney.
Another removes waste.
Where would they be
without law suits
and garbage trucks?
Perhaps within the grand
Grand Canyon
legally wasting time.

BUDDHA'S BREW

A half empty beer bottle
dares me to stand
on my head.

POSTCARD TO THE EPHESIANS

If everything is everything
and nothing is nothing,
holiness is being at one
with the hole.

RELATIVE CONCERNS

The wind and I are brothers
seeking reasons
to blow each other away.

PLANETARY PEACE

Imagine a world voluntarily disarmed.
There's a way that could peacefully occur.
In a piece of your imagination.

ANNIVERSARY

Woodpeckers peck at bark for food.
Machine guns peck at people.
A year passes and the sky
remains the same.

HUNTING

This season I had a buck clear in my sites.
I pulled nothing. He did nothing.
We both just walked away.
Did I help preserve an unendangered species?
Is he looking forward to winter?
Might we co-write a novel,
Never Mind Minding?

THEORIES OF RELATIVITY

A goldfish thinks its bowl
is the universe.
We think the universe
is our bowl.
Monks reflect on their reflections.
Everything is everything
is it not?

BYE LINES

When a fish is caught
it drowns in air.
Whales wonder how far
we can swim?

SUB URBS

Nothing says nothing
like lawns.

MEASURES

Georgia has the largest mosquitoes in North America.
Brooklyn has the fastest rodents.
The Bronx River is the shallowest in the nation.
The Grand Canyon suffers from massive chronic depression.
The Mafia is the smallest college fraternity.
Its members are all business majors.
Despite mothers insistence, we are born with limited potential.
We learn that on our first date.

THREE ZEN REMARKS

The wisdom of the desert is the desert.
Are paths not trend upon paths?
Rain descends, leaves drift,
your intention?

ROLLING STONED

When you're deeply drunk you forget
that music and memories
can't be grasped.
You remember you believed
you would write
a novel novel.

CELL TO CELL

Rock to jazz, married to single,
priest to atheist,
flesh to fertilizer.
Then talk it all over
with the other guys
in jail.

RECALL

To remember is useful to pass examinations,
celebrate anniversaries, relate to your analyst,
argue, dispute, agree to dispute,
find your way home
and sense there never is one.
Times for prayer and deflection.

ALAS, A LACK

Last week I received a memo from heaven
stating my guardian angel has resigned.
A replacement will be found but it's going
to take some time.
Too many people, too few angels.
They admit they must modernize
current recruitment techniques.
Until then, I'm on my own.
Their best advice for getting by
is to hang loose, pray
and never trust a person
whose middle name is Harvey.

EXPEDITIONS

There's the Appalachian Trail and the
Bronx River Parkway.
Both require valid passports and proof
of good intention.
The natives exchange whiskey and grass
for valid currency and can be violent
if exploited.
They speak languages that are only now
beginning to be fully understood.
Upon return you might write a book
describing the adventure or be featured
in an issue of *National Geographic*.
Where next to go? Confession?

FAST TALK

Yesterday I had lunch with a monk who was digesting his fast.
We reviewed what we knew about the early fathers of the church.
None of them would believe the church has had to last this long.
Certainly the Second Coming should have come by now.
That it hasn't is more than disconcerting.
We decided to become students of history:
The study of rites and wrongs.
Only later did I realize what really had occurred:
It had been a close encounter
of the very first kind.

END TIMES

When the universe
finally freezes,
when everything,
everywhere is cold,
God will be
the memory
of heat.

ABOUT THE AUTHOR

Michael Maiello has served as Executive Director of Catholic Family And Community Services, Diocese Of Paterson, New Jersey and as Paterson's Diocesan Director Of Social Services. He holds degrees from St. John's University, City University Of New York and St. John's University School Of Law. He has written essays and articles on civic and social justice issues. His book-length poetic publications include *Paths And Approaches* and *Sacred Moments, Holy Days.*

A number of the poems here have appeared in *The Edge; The Elm; The Hudson Valley Journal; Lighthouse; New Moon Poetry; The Pen; The Poet's Way, and Sojourners.*